ADA LOVELACE

WHO WAS...?

ADA LOVELACE

THE COMPUTER WIZARD OF VICTORIAN ENGLAND

BY **LUCY LETHBRIDGE**

ILLUSTRATED BY **JAMES NUNN**

✱ SHORT BOOKS

First published in 2003 by
Short Books
15 Highbury Terrace
London N5 1UP

10 9 8 7 6 5 4 3 2 1

A CIP catalogue record for this book
is available from the British Library.

ISBN 1-904095-52-6

Printed in Great Britain by
Bookmarque Ltd, Croydon, Surrey

$$v0 = m$$
$$v1 = n$$

$$x + 1000 + y$$
$$m + 7$$

$$aRb$$
$$(\exists x) \quad aRx \times Rb$$
$$(\exists x, y) \quad aRx \times Eyy Rb$$

$$\sum_{k\,0}^{kn} \binom{k\,n}{k} - Ln$$

$$x + y =$$
$$\pi + 10$$

CHAPTER ONE

Late on a Saturday afternoon in the winter of 1833, a young woman with an eager, long-nosed face and dark, observing eyes walked into the drawing-room of Charles Babbage's house in Dorset Street in London, dressed in a bright-red dress. She was accompanied by an angular, sad-looking woman dressed unbecomingly all in black.

Ada Augusta Byron, who was 18 years old and brilliantly clever, and her mother, Annabella, Lady Byron, were not alone; a crowd of visitors had

also come to see the strange figure standing in a dancer's pose on a pedestal in the centre of the room. The dancer was shining dully in the candle-light, as though she were made of pieces of moon-light stitched together; in fact she was made of metal.

Ada elbowed her way to the front, anxious to have a good view of Charles Babbage's latest invention, the 'Silver Dancer'. For a while the dancer stood with her head lowered, then she raised her face and turned precisely upon one leg, the other one rising up behind her in a graceful pirouette. Her breast heaved gently as she lifted her silk petticoat. Her lovely face turned slowly towards her audience, her eyes fixed on them in a blank, unsmiling stare. On her outstretched hand rested a tiny bird whose wings flapped delicately, its bewildered head turning from side to side.

The metallic tick-tocking of the dancer's clock-work mechanism was drowned out by the excited 'oohs' and 'aahs' of the crowd. Someone whispered, 'She's exactly like life.' And, for a moment, it was possible to believe that the Silver Dancer was indeed real. Then, just as suddenly as she had sprung into action, she stopped moving, her leg suspended in mid-air, her eyes blindly turned towards the wall, the wings of her bird arrested in mid-flutter.

With a flourish, Charles Babbage appeared from behind the pedestal and produced a large key, which he turned theatrically two or three times in the dancer's back. Her springs once again coiled for action, she cranked slowly back into life and began her never-ending cycle of pirouettes.

Ada was fascinated. She wanted to work out how the Silver Dancer moved. She was not impressed by the beauty of the dancer's face or the elegance of her pirouettes. She thought of beauty as the sleek precision with which the cogs and springs moved inside the dancer's sculpted frame.

As the other visitors began to wander away, Ada stayed there in front of the pedestal, transfixed – quite unaware that she herself was now under observation by an elderly dowager standing with another woman at the edge of the room.

'My dear, you see that girl in the red dress standing by the Silver Dancer?' the dowager hissed excitedly to her companion. 'You *must* know who she is. She's the daughter of Lord Byron!'

CHAPTER TWO

Ada Augusta Byron was born on 10th December 1815. She never knew her father – the 'Mad, bad, and dangerous to know' Lord Byron – because her parents separated when she was only a year old. They had been a very odd couple.

Lord Byron, with his long, dark curls, his fingers covered with rings, and his fierce energy was desperately attractive, despite having been born with a club foot that made him limp. Mothers covered their daughters' eyes when they saw him approaching for they feared that a single glance at Byron was all that was needed to fall hopelessly in love with him. He was rumoured to have had lots of lovers.

He was a superb athlete, a great boxer and fencer, and he was famous for having dared to swim across the Hellespont (a five-mile stretch of choppy water that connects the Aegean Sea with the Sea of Marmara which is now called the Dardanelles). He was also England's most famous Romantic poet; people queued to buy his latest books, which were all bestsellers.

Annabella, Lady Byron, in contrast, was extremely well-behaved. In fact her enemies (and she had a few) said she was prim and self-satisfied; her husband, before they were married, nicknamed her the 'Princess of Parallelograms' because she was so infuriatingly logical. To begin with, he admired her stern, unbending principles and her insistence on facts over fantasy. He even

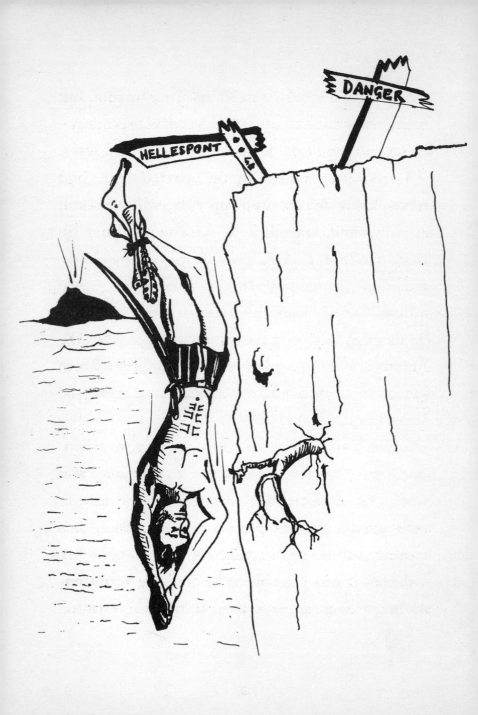

thought she might be a good influence on him. But he soon got tired of his wife's reproving sermons – he had no intention of giving up his wicked ways.

Lord and Lady Byron parted on bad terms: Lady Byron swept up Ada, who was still a baby, and travelled to Kirkby Mallory in Leicestershire to live with her parents. Soon afterwards, Lord Byron sailed for the Continent, taking his beloved dog, a Newfoundland called Boatswain, with him as a companion. But the Byrons did not lose touch completely – they wrote letters to each other about Ada and how she should be educated.

At that time, girls like Ada with rich, aristocratic parents were usually taught at home, and were not expected to learn very much except drawing, dancing and playing the piano. But Ada's mother wanted her daughter to be as unlike her father as it was possible to be, and she surrounded her with governesses and tutors who ensured that her life was strictly regimented from the moment she woke up until it was time for bed. Not a day went by in which Ada did not learn something. The only subject about which she was taught nothing at all was poetry, because her mother, after her experience with Lord Byron, thought that too much poetry was bad for the character.

CHAPTER THREE

In 1824, when Ada was eight years old, Lord Byron fell ill with a fever while fighting in the war in Greece. He had joined up with the rebels against the Turkish empire, which then ruled Greece and much of the Middle East. When he died at Missolonghi in July, aged just 36, the entire nation was plunged into mourning for its favourite badly behaved poet.

Lord Byron's body was brought back to England in an ivory casket. It was then taken from London to Nottinghamshire in an elaborate funeral procession so that he could be buried in the Byron family's vault in the churchyard at Hucknall Torkard. All along the way, in every village, church bells tolled and local people gathered at the roadside, taking off their hats and bowing their heads in respect as the 47 carriages with their teams of black-plumed horses swept by, Byron's beloved dogs limping along sadly beside them (Boatswain had died years earlier).

At Kirkby Mallory, on the day of the funeral, all the windows were open in the summer heat; the only sound was the buzzing of bees and the occasional swish of the maids' long skirts as they scurried between rooms carrying chicken broth and cold compresses. Upstairs, Lady Byron had shut herself in her bedroom, from which came the sound of loud weeping. In the drawing-room a large portrait of Lord Byron was veiled by a green-velvet curtain. It had been covered over ever since Ada was a baby, and so she had never seen the handsome face of her father, dressed for having his picture painted in Albanian costume, his head swathed in an exotic turban.

Ada spent the afternoon sitting on the lawn with her cat Puff on her lap, reading her favourite book, *Bingley's Useful Knowledge*. She was feeling very hot and sticky in the heat, and thought how unfair it was that she had been told she must wear the new black dress and bonnet that had been made specially for her as soon as her mother heard of Lord Byron's death.

The dress, made of itchy black bombazine was tight in the bodice and had a very long skirt, under which she had to wear black petticoats. In those days, whenever someone died, their family wore black for at least a year in honour of their memory. Lady Byron, who always liked to make a point, remained in black for the rest of her life.

But it was difficult, thought Ada, to mourn

someone you had never known. She had no memories of her father. His name was hardly ever mentioned at Kirkby Mallory; and whenever one of her mother's guests made the mistake of mentioning poetry or poets, or Greece, or even husbands, Ada had noticed that a tense silence would follow. Once, Ada had asked her mother about 'Papa', but had been answered with such silent fury that she resolved never to ask again.

On the day of his funeral, her mother stayed in her room, refusing to talk to anyone. For once, Ada was allowed to spend the day doing exactly what she liked – reading.

Her lessons usually began almost as soon as she got up – at six o'clock in the morning – and went on till suppertime. And that was every day of the week except Sundays when the house was very quiet and the only book Ada was allowed to read was the Bible. Her governess was expected to teach her French, German, geography, scripture,

needlework, drawing, music and dancing, while special tutors came to the house to give her lessons in Latin, Greek, algebra, mathematics, geometry, calculus and metaphysics (the kind of philosophy that looks into the existence of God and why things are the way they are).

Even at the age of eight, Ada could solve in a flash problems such as: 'If 750 men are allowed 2,250 rations of bread per month, how many rations will a garrison of 1,200 men require?'

She was fascinated by numbers, equations and calculations; and she thought that solving an especially difficult mathematical problem was much more important than painting a picture or writing a story.

When Ada was ten, her mother took her on the Grand Tour, to see the ancient towns of France and Germany and the paintings of Michelangelo, Leonardo da Vinci and Raphael in Italy. They were abroad for a whole year, and spent a lot of time rattling down bumpy roads in horse-drawn coaches.

Ada saw mountains for the first time, glaciers, huge lakes and the Mediterranean Sea. She observed scorpions, fireflies and ant-hills in the garden of their villa in Naples in southern Italy; and heard the munching of locusts in the fields. In her bedroom she saw emerald lizards scampering up the curtains; and at night she was kept awake by croaking black and green frogs. Everything was so different from what she knew at Kirkby Mallory that she saw it all with startling clarity, recording in her diary all that she had seen in exact detail.

She was particularly excited by Lake Geneva, a deep sheet of blue water, which lies like a brimming cup beneath the Swiss mountains. Looking out from the window of the hotel where they were staying, she noticed that the lake did not always glimmer in the same way. Under a full moon, there were two kinds of silver light shimmering on the water: where the water was calm, it was a 'dead' silver; where the water was rippling in the wind, the silver seemed to be 'living'.

No one had told her that her father Lord Byron had also visited the lake and had stayed in the mysterious Castle Chillon, a sinister place that juts out over the water. While there, he had written a famous poem – 'The Prisoner of Chillon' – about a prisoner chained up in its dungeons, thousands of feet underneath the lake. He had carved his own name deep into the stone walls of the castle. But this, too, Ada never knew.

CHAPTER FOUR

When they returned to England, Ada and her mother moved to a big house near Canterbury in Kent, called Bifrons. But almost as soon as they arrived, Lady Byron, who was a bit of a hypochondriac and always complained of never feeling quite well, set off again for Europe to visit the spa towns in Germany, Austria and Switzerland for her health. There, she could drink the spring waters and breathe the clear Alpine air.

Ada was left at home alone with her governess, Miss Stamp. She led a very solitary life, with no brothers and sisters, and no school friends with whom she could play. One afternoon, sitting in the schoolroom with the windows open and hearing only the sounds of the sheep grazing in the parkland beyond the house and garden, Miss Stamp read aloud to Ada the Greek myth of Daedalus and Icarus, who escaped from their Cretan prison on wings made of feathers and wax. Icarus, taken over by the excitement of flying, flew too near the sun: the wax on his wings melted and he crashed to earth.

'Pride comes before a fall,' remarked Miss Stamp reprovingly. Ada, however, was thinking that it was pretty obvious that wax was an unsuitable method of adhesive if you wanted to fly close to the sun. It seemed to her that you could make a machine do anything you wanted – if only you thought it through properly first.

That night, Ada heard a mysterious crunching sound that was coming from under her bed. She lay awake for a while, listening and wondering what it could be. Eventually, she braved the darkness to find out what it was. When she knelt down to look under the bed, there was Puff, eyes gleaming in the light of her candle, chewing energetically on the bones of a dead bird that he had dragged in from the garden.

Ada reached under the bed and pulled out an entire wing, that had survived untouched. She examined it closely. Its filigree of bones had a tapestry of feathers sewn over it. Each portion was equipped to catch the breeze and ride the edge of a wind wave. At that moment, it occurred to her that it should be perfectly possible to create a pair of human wings; and she determined that she would be the first person to design and make a human flying machine. She called her idea 'Flyology'.

Next morning she got up very early and set to work clearing out the stable so that she could have

her own laboratory in which she could do her Flyology experiments.

'Flyology?' asked Miss Stamp nervously, as she watched Ada heaving saddles, bridles and horse-bits out into the yard.

'Yes,' said Ada, nailing a wind-current chart to the stable wall. 'Apart from a comprehensive volume on the anatomy of birds, I need oiled silk, stiff wire and graph paper. But no wax,' she added, as a joke.

Miss Stamp retreated into the house. She went into the drawing-room, lay on the sofa and read her favourite passages from the volume of Lord Byron's poems that she kept hidden in a secret pocket sewn into her skirts. Then she tweaked back the corner of the green-velvet curtain that covered his picture.

'Mad, bad, and dangerous to know,' she sighed.

For the next year, Ada spent every moment she was not being supervised by Miss Stamp in her laboratory, making calculations and doing experiments on the wings of the birds that Puff brought in from the garden. She wrote to her mother every day, telling her everything about her progress in Flyology. Sometimes, she felt so nearly able to fly that she could imagine herself swooping up into the sky and looking down on the rolling patchwork world of fields and rivers below.

Ada reckoned that if the weight of a single bird could be carried by its wings, then it must be perfectly possible to devise wings that would carry humans. The trick was to calculate the size of a bird's wing in relation to its body, and then to work out the exact proportions needed for a human pair of wings. She spent hours studying flight patterns and poring over diagrams of birds' anatomy.

The next step, after making a person airborne would be to create an even larger pair of wings that would bear the weight of a steam engine. Ada thought that this would prove useful to the Royal Mail. A winged flyer, thought Ada, could deliver letters for a whole region by herself with a small bag containing a compass and a map. In her letters to her mother Ada began to call herself the 'Carrier Pidgeon'.

CHAPTER FIVE

In the autumn of 1827, Lady Byron eventually returned from the Continent. She was worried that Ada had become obsessed with Flyology and was spending too much time by herself in her laboratory. She had decided that it was time Ada stopped dreaming about machines and instead learnt about things that would be useful and moral.

When Miss Stamp left to work for another family, she was replaced by a whole team of tutors, who were expected to instil in Ada self-control, self-reliance, and an ability to think for herself.

Not long afterwards Lady Byron and Ada moved to Fordhook, a mansion, white as a sugar-cube, at Mortlake, which in Ada's day was a quiet village on the River Thames. Lady Byron invited her three unmarried female friends to live with them, hoping that they would be a good influence on her wayward daughter. But Ada felt that they were spying on her, looming over everything she did like the Furies of Greek myth. If she stayed out too long riding on her horse Sylph, they reported it to her mother; if she talked too much, they told her that she must learn to control herself; if she didn't talk, they asked her what the matter was. Ada began to feel that even her private thoughts were not safe from their constant scrutiny.

Ada, who was now 16, hated being watched all the time by the Three Furies (as she called them in

secret), and being expected always to use her time doing what her mother thought was useful. And she was lonely.

One day in November 1832, when the trees were furred with frost and the lawns were brushed with silver, a young man walked up the Fordhook drive, wearing a threadbare coat with patches on the elbows and a thin woollen scarf. William Turner, who was 18, was a university student living in a rented room in Mortlake with a fierce landlady to whom he paid a few shillings a week for a hard bed and a breakfast of thin porridge. His allowance from his father was not nearly enough to pay for his tuition and his lodgings, so Lady Byron had employed him to teach Ada shorthand.

William approached Fordhook nervously. Inside his pocket, he carried a well-thumbed copy of his favourite book, Lord Byron's poems. William wondered what she would be like, the daughter of Lord Byron. He had been told that she was a prodigy, a brilliant mathematician who had lessons from the finest experts in the country. He wondered whether Ada would be beautiful, like her father and if he might fall in love with her. He rather hoped so. Like his hero, Lord Byron, William was a Romantic, and in secret, at night, he wrote his own poetry.

As he walked up the drive, he could hear coming from inside the house the melancholy thrumming of a guitar and plaintive singing. A face with a drooping moustache looked mournfully out of the window. William was thrilled; this was exactly what he expected from the home of Byron's daughter.

The music, however, was nothing to do with Ada. She was sitting on an over-stuffed sofa in the drawing-room reading Dionysius Lardner's *Analytical Treatise on Plane and Spherical Trigonometry*. She took little notice of the family portraits that were crammed together on all four walls, and had never asked about the largest picture above the fireplace, which was covered over by the green-velvet curtain.

She was not nervous at the thought of meeting her new tutor – she had seen so many come and go on her mother's whims – but she did wonder what William would be like, hoping that he would at least be younger than her other teachers.

When William first saw Ada, she was wearing a vivid crimson dress with green buttons (Ada, unlike her mother, always liked to wear bright colours). He thought that she was not exactly beautiful, but her face was interesting, the kind you remember. Her large brown eyes and dark hair resembled her father. She seemed to him organised and energetic, but very bossy, showing him a timetable of her classes and telling him that she needed no less than three hours a week of shorthand.

'I like to know how things work,' she

announced to William, looking up from her book on trigonometry. 'I cannot bear not to be able to explain things: that is why I love mathematics – it has answers.'

Fordhook seemed to William to be full of Ada's teachers: Count Urrea, the man with the droopy moustache who taught her the guitar; Miss D'Espourria, the harp teacher; Augustus de Morgan, who taught her logic; Dr Frend, an expert in mathematics; Dr King, her moral and spiritual teacher who believed that Ada needed to be protected from her obsessions and enthusiasms; and Professor Faia, who tried to teach Ada how to sing. It surprised William that they all treated Ada as though she were a naughty child who without their continual vigilance would play truant and fall into ruin.

'I was wondering,' he asked politely one afternoon, 'what's behind the green curtain?'

'It's a portrait of my father,' Ada told him

brusquely. 'But I've never seen it.'

'Well you don't need to see a picture of Lord Byron when you have his poetry,' said William.

Ada looked at him in surprise. 'I wouldn't know – I've never read any of my father's poems.'

'Not one?'

'No – I never read poetry. Dr King thinks that encouraging the imagination leads to too much passion and a lack of self-control.'

William looked at Ada in amazement. She had never seen her father's face, and she had never read a line of his poems. 'But poetry is so beautiful,' he told her.

'That,' said Ada, 'is how I think about mathematics. Every time I solve a mathematical problem, it makes a lovely shape in my head.'

CHAPTER SIX

One afternoon, after he had been teaching Ada for about a fortnight, William was invited to stay for dinner, which in a large house like Fordhook in the 1830s would have been a grand affair: lobster jelly, creamed pigs' trotters, boiled carp, pigeon pie, braised mutton and lots of different junkets, jellies, custards and ices. William could not afford to eat much more than porridge for breakfast and muffins for the rest of the day, with an occasional glass of ale, so he was always ravenous.

At the dinner table, Ada was seated next to Lady Byron and opposite the Three Furies, who were anxious to supervise Ada's conversation. Further down the table were her other tutors: Ada was never free from the constant watchful eye of her teachers.

William watched as Lady Byron piled up her plate with greasy slabs of mutton, announcing to her guests, 'This is the Golden Fleece of meats.' His appetite suddenly disappeared. No wonder, he thought, everyone at Fordhook always seemed to have upset stomachs. No surprise, either, that Ada was often liverish and bad-tempered. Her mother had told him it was because she had no self-control, but William guessed it was because she was sick of eating indigestible mutton.

Although the food was a disappointment, William was entranced by the conversation. Dr Frend, the mathematician, had just spent the day in London, where he had called on Charles

Babbage in the hope of being invited to see his miraculous machines. He was so amazed by them that he could not stop talking about the Silver Dancer – and the even more wondrous Difference Engine, an invention so extraordinary that, said Dr Frend, 'it really could change the world'.

'It's not as big as you might think,' he told William. 'It's a compact group of metal tubes. But the remarkable thing is that it appears to be able to think for itself.'

'That's impossible,' said Dr King. 'Such a thing would be quite against God's law.'

'But it is all based on mathematical principles – there is nothing ungodly about it,' retorted Dr Frend. 'God created the universe to operate by certain rules of nature, after all.

'Babbage's Difference Engine,' he explained to William, 'is able to undertake complex mathematical calculations. All the operator has to do is to set it to do them. Calculations that would take a human mind some time to work out can be done in an instant.'

Ada, who was ignoring the Three Furies beside her in an effort to overhear what Dr Frend was telling William, exclaimed: 'But that would mean that the operator need know nothing at all about the method of calculation – the machine could do it all for him.'

'Indeed,' said Dr Frend, 'it's a machine with a brain made of cogs and levers that, when it comes to calculations at least, is as good as the human brain and far more accurate. After all, a machine like this is never tired or unwell or out of sorts. As long as it has the pattern imprinted into it, it is always able to come up with the right answers – which is more than you can say for human beings.'

'But what,' interrupted Lady Byron, 'is the purpose of this machine?'

'To work out all the calculations which take us human beings hours of toil,' said Dr Frend.

'Think of mathematical tables – they are important for astronomers, navigators, engineers, bankers, insurance brokers and sailors. If a navigational table contains just one single mistake, it can cause a shipwreck.'

'I know,' broke in Ada. 'Dionysius Lardner once went through 40 volumes of number tables and found 3,700 mistakes.'

'Quite right,' said Dr Frend. 'If a machine were able to do all these calculations without any mistakes – think how much time we would have left to do other things, and how many sailors' lives would be saved.'

'So why isn't this machine in use already?' asked one of the Furies, bossily.

'Aaaah. Poor Babbage,' said Dr Frend. 'The Difference Engine is only part of the whole machine. He is still trying to raise the funds from the government to complete it. Who knows if we will see in our lifetimes the finished engine. But imagine it – a future where machines may do our calculations for us; may be capable even of playing chess.'

'Preposterous!' spluttered Dr King. 'It is quite unnatural – human beings are designed for suffering and hardship. Think of what the world would be like if all our hard work was done by machines – it would go to the dogs.'

'Idleness and sloth!' agreed his thin, bony wife, who was sitting next to him.

But, from across the table, William saw that Ada's eyes were shining with excitement.

*

That night, Ada couldn't sleep. What Dr Frend had told them about Charles Babbage and his extraordinary inventions had thrilled her. If it were possible to invent a machine that worked as well as the human brain, what limits were there to

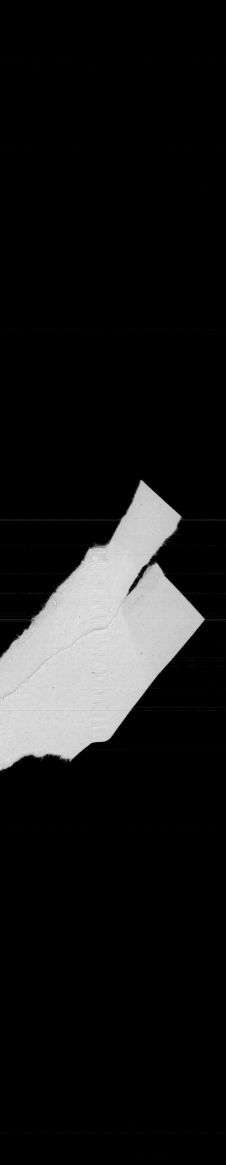

the future? She knew that she had to see the Difference Engine for herself, and meet the man who had created it.

But when she asked Lady Byron for permission to take the carriage into London, she was told that it would be 'bad for your health' to travel to the grimy, smoke-ridden city. In any case, it was 'inappropriate' for her to visit a man's house by herself; she was 'far too young'.

Ada confided in William. 'It's so unfair. I want to see the Difference Engine more than anything in the world.' But November passed into December, and still her mother refused to let her go.

Then one day, Ada asked William, 'Where would you like to go if you could choose anywhere in the world?'

William thought for a minute, before replying, 'Newstead Abbey.'

Ada was silent. She had heard of the ruined

abbey in Nottinghamshire – it had been her father's home until he had had to sell it after spending his fortune on high living and gambling. But her mother had always refused to tell her anything about it.

'What's it like?' she said at last.

So William told her the story of the strange, haunted abbey in the middle of Sherwood Forest. Lord Byron had never had enough money to keep the rain out of Newstead. Gradually the abbey and the house attached to it had fallen into ruin. Inside, the wallpaper had come away in strips and water had washed away the gleam on the gold-painted griffins, eagles and coronets. But the ancient oak woods were still there, and the bottomless lake, and the mock castles on the lakeside from where the Byrons as children had held mock battles.

William described the hideous faces of the gargoyles under the roof; the constant drip, drip of water in the rain-sodden dungeons; and, of course, the mysterious black-cloaked figure that Byron had woken up to find sitting on the end of his bed, glaring at him.

Ada listened carefully, storing up the images in her memory – in the place where she hoarded the few clues that she had gathered about her father.

CHAPTER SEVEN

By the end of January 1833, it was bitterly cold. The edges of the River Thames had turned to thin, creaking ice. Ada asked if she could skate on the lake in Mortlake, which was frozen solid. William went with her, though, inevitably, they were accompanied by the Three Furies: it would have been unthinkable in those days for an unmarried girl to go skating, alone, with a young man almost her own age.

The Furies were too frightened to step out on to the ice, so they stood on the edge, looking on disapprovingly as William and Ada skated round and round in circles, scratching figures of eight in the ice.

'Look at the shapes!' cried Ada in excitement. 'Can you see how everything has an order to it? It is like mathematics, finding the pattern behind things.'

Watching Ada, William felt a jolt in his stomach that was nothing to do with skating. He wondered if it was love. He was sure it must be – it was a Byronic feeling, a moment from a poem.

That night, he could not sleep, tossing and turning just like, he imagined, a Romantic hero. He wondered what Ada would say if he told her that he was in love with her. Would she laugh at him? Or would she sigh happily and tell him that she loved him too?

Next morning, as soon as Ada arrived in the schoolroom for her shorthand lesson, William went down on one knee (as he had heard was customary in such situations) and declared himself to be passionately, desperately in love with her.

To his surprise, Ada simply said, bossily: 'When we are married, we can live at your house.'

'But I don't live in a house – I live at Mrs Spatchett's in the village.'

'I don't care where we live,' said Ada, 'as long as it's not here.'

'But what will we do for money?'

'What does money matter?'

Poor William began to feel worried – Ada had no idea what life was like if you were poor.

'I'll bring my horse Sylph, of course,' Ada went on brightly.

'That really wouldn't be a good idea – there's no room at Mrs Spatchett's.'

'Nonsense – even a really tiny house will have room for a horse.'

As the days went on and Ada continued in

this blunt, business-like fashion, William felt as though he was trapped inside a snowball hurtling down a hill – and he couldn't stop it. This was not at all like the romances written about by Lord Byron.

But Ada had found a new enthusiasm, and she thought of nothing else but how they could escape. She decided that on the appointed day William would return home to Mrs Spatchett's at four o'clock as usual. Then he would sneak back to Fordhook as soon as it was dark and wait in the stables. While the household were having dinner, Ada would make some excuse to leave the dining-room; run upstairs, collect the parcel of clothes and books she had wrapped up in a silk shawl, let herself out of the house by the kitchen door and go to the stables. By the time anyone in the house realised that they were gone, they would be on their way to London – and married.

At least that was the idea. But elopements –

despite what is written about them in poetry and novels – rarely go as planned. Ada had forgotten how long dinner usually took at Fordhook, and how difficult it was to find an opportunity to leave the room without acting suspiciously. On the evening that she had chosen for their escape, she was still waiting for the butler to serve the custard cups at 8.30pm, two hours later than the time she had promised to meet William at the stables.

She had also underestimated the spying abilities of the Furies, who simply didn't take their eyes off her for a second; Miss Montgomery, in particular, looked as though she knew something was up, and Ada began to wonder if the old cat had been reading her diaries.

William was shivering and about to give up when at last Ada ran out of the house clutching her bag of precious belongings. Minutes later, as they were about to reach the garden gate to freedom, a beam of light shone into their faces. Dr

King was advancing upon them from across the
lawn carrying a lantern.

'Come out both of you,' he boomed. 'Lady
Byron orders you to come out this instant.'

It was all over – almost before it had begun.
William was marched back to Mrs Spatchett's and
Ada never saw him again. She was locked in her

room for weeks, with only sermons from Dr King to look forward to and reproachful looks from her mother. The Three Furies called in on her from time to time, looking unbearably smug.

Crushed, but not quite defeated, Ada decided that being in love with numbers was better than falling in love with a man. As Dr King put it: 'Focus and self-discipline are the twin pillars of a fruitful and virtuous life.' From now on, Ada determined, she would devote herself to hard work and becoming a good person; she would master her passions by concentrating her mind on logical calculations and the beauty of numbers.

CHAPTER EIGHT

In 1833, a century before the invention of television, and before radio, films or CD-players, the most fashionable entertainment in London was looking at new inventions. Crowds of people gathered to see the first electric telegraph sending tapped messages down a crackling line. Many visited London University Hospital to see Dr John Elliotson performing his strange but extraordinary acts of Mesmerism.

With the assistance of two strange, wild sisters called the Okeys, Elliotson demonstrated how –

using magnets and electric currents – he could make them become completely still and even stick pins in their necks without them feeling any pain. These performances were so popular that there was barely room for all the gawpers to squeeze in.

But now that Merlin's Mechanical Museum – the home of clockwork magic, where clockwork birds fluttering in cages and dancing elephants could be seen – had closed, the best entertainment in London was to be found at Charles Babbage's house on Saturday afternoons.

He had invented shoes with hinged flaps that could walk on water, a method of delivering messages using overhead cables, a 'black box' for checking the condition of railway tracks, and special lights to enable communication from on land with ships at sea.

He had designed 'speaking tubes' that could link London and Liverpool, a diving-bell, a machine that played noughts and crosses, and a submarine propelled by compressed air. But his finest and most famous achievement was the Difference Engine.

When Ada and her mother arrived at the house in Dorset Street for the first time on that Saturday afternoon in 1833, Ada was fascinated by the Silver Dancer twirling sadly in her endless mechanical pirouette. But it was what she saw next that would change her forever; a moment in time that for Ada was a leap in understanding, a sudden realisation of what she was meant to do with the rest of her life.

There, in the corner of the room, was a shiny object, the size of a largish travelling trunk. It looked like nothing Ada had ever seen before; she later described it as being like the inside of a giant clock. The Difference Engine, or 'Thinking Machine' as Ada liked to call it, was a compressed knot of hundreds of interlocking cogs and wheels that sparkled in the candlelight. The wheels, Ada noticed, were all numbered on their brass rims from 0 to 9.

*

'Do you know,' whispered a voice in Ada's ear, 'the British government has lost £2.3 million as a result of errors in mathematical tables? And do you think they are prepared to pay decent money to develop my Difference Engine – to save countless hours and countless poor slaves working their brains to the bone making the calculations that could be done in a matter of seconds by my machine?'

Ada turned round to see a smallish man with a furious expression on his face.

'The answer is NO, emphatically NO.'

Charles Babbage was renowned for his irascible temper.

'I have spent ten years working on the

Difference Engine,' he shouted at Ada. 'And all I have completed is a portion of it – a mere one-seventh – 2,000 separate parts. If it were completed, it would the most complex machine ever built.

'It needs to have 25,000 parts,' he continued. 'Each one precisely crafted so that they are all identical down to the last detail. When it is finished, the engine will be eight foot high, seven foot long and three foot deep... IF I finish it.'

'Will you show me how it works?' interrupted Ada.

'In precisely five minutes the demonstration will begin,' answered Babbage, leaping nimbly over to his machine and taking up a position by a large handle attached to its side. The other visitors, drawn in by the sound of his ranting voice, crowded round the Difference Engine.

He paused for a moment, and then pulled the handle on its side. 'I want you to watch carefully, fixing your eyes on these brass wheels on the machine. As you will observe, they are all set at 0.'

Everyone leaned forward. The wheels that they could see were indeed all engraved with the number zero.

'I will now begin to turn this handle,' said Babbage, 'and you will note please that the numbers will all begin to change.'

There was the smooth sound of well-oiled metal turning – and on each of the wheels appeared the figure '2'. Babbage went on turning the handle and a '4' appeared, then a '6' and an '8'. Over and over they turned – 10, 12, 14, 16, and so on until they reached the hundreds – 102, 104, 106. The numbers were changing according to a simple rule: add two.

A few of the onlookers grew restless; a woman in a feathered headdress gave a yawn. This machine of Babbage's didn't seem so interesting after all. On and on, it repeated its infinite procession of numbers. Then, suddenly, just as his audience began to drift away, the wheels showed a different number altogether – 379.

A man called out, triumphantly. 'Your machine's made a mistake, Babbage – it should be 180 written on the wheels.'

The crowd sniggered. But Babbage looked delighted: 'I thank you, sir, for your sharp observation, but there is no mistake. I knew that the number 379 would come up after the number 178, and how did I know?' He patted his machine lovingly. 'Because I deliberately set the machine to add on the number 201 after 89 repetitions and thus to leap to the number 379.

'You think that I have broken a rule, but in fact this machine has stuck absolutely to the rules that I established for it.'

Ada stood and watched, lost in thought. It was the most exciting day of her life. She understood that she had witnessed something that would change the world.

As she and her mother were leaving, Charles Babbage went up to them and pointed to the Silver Dancer.

'Isn't she adorable? I met her first when I was seven years old when my mother took me to Merlin's Mechanical Museum in Burlington Arcade. She turned her lovely metal head and rolled her eyes at me, and I fell in love with her. Years later, after Merlin's closed down, I bought her at a sale; she was in pieces in a box so I brought her home and put her together again.'

Then he asked Ada, 'Do you know about mathematics, my dear? Algebra, logarithms, square roots and calculus.'

'Yes,' she answered, with some dignity. She did not tell him that she was considered by many (including herself) to be a mathematical genius.

CHAPTER NINE

Ada went back to Dorset Street several times without her mother, who, now that she had met Babbage and recognised his single-minded devotion to his machines, realised that no harm could come to Ada's reputation by going there without a chaperone.

Babbage was obsessed with trying to build the next stage of his Difference Engine, which he called the Analytical Engine. He had made all the necessary calculations, and drafted the designs, but he simply did not have enough money to pay for its hundreds of cogs and wheels to be specially manufactured. Only Ada truly understood how the Analytical Engine could revolutionise the way that everything was calculated, from the proportions necessary to build a flying machine to working out how much scarlet silk to buy for a full-length ballgown.

'My dear Miss Byron, there is absolutely no pleasing the English,' Babbage told Ada one afternoon. 'If you say that you have made a machine for peeling the potato, they will tell you it is impossible. If you peel a potato with it before their eyes, they will say it is useless, because it will not slice a pineapple.'

Ada was determined to show him that she understood, and for the next two years she devoted herself to making calculations and solving complex mathematical problems, preparing herself to become Babbage's assistant.

Such was Ada's dedication to her cause that

Lady Byron began to wonder at her own wisdom in having allowed her daughter to become so embroiled with Babbage and his creation. Ada had never had what one might regard as a normal social life, even for a girl of that epoch: she was far too eccentric and brainy for that. All the same, her mother reckoned, she ought to have some contact with her peers. At this rate, Ada would never get married; after all, she was almost 20, well past the age when daughters of aristocratic families were expected to have found a husband. Although she would inherit from her mother when she died, she would not have enough money to last her lifetime.

Lady Byron began to look for a suitable man to whom she could introduce Ada. He had to be rich; because Ada was used to living in a big house with all the comforts that money could offer. But her mother knew that he would also have to be very intelligent so that her clever daughter would not be bored. She launched Ada in society, presenting her at Court and ensuring that she was invited to as many balls as possible.

Ada, though not interested in fashion, loved dressing up, and on one occasion went to a fancy-dress ball as a stick of maize, with a head-dress of cornflowers and silver heads of corn under a silver fringe. It was not only her dresses that shocked people; Ada always insisted on speaking in a very loud voice – and about subjects not often discussed at parties, such as algebra and Babbage's calculations for his Analytical Engine.

Despite this, as the daughter of the infamous Lord Byron, she was always a popular guest, and in the spring of 1835 she was invited to a country-house party in Warwickshire where she met William Lovelace, also known as Lord King. William was ten years older than Ada, but he owned two country estates, at Ockham Park in Surrey and Ashley Combe, by the sea in Somerset, and was solid and dependable. Lady Byron was thrilled.

What she didn't know then was that he had been a bit of an adventurer, living for more than a year on the Greek island of Corfu. He showed Ada a portrait of himself dressed in Corfu's national dress – an embroidered waistcoat and turban – with a curving dagger in his belt, very like the portrait of Lord Byron behind the green-velvet curtain, which, of course, Ada had never seen.

William also liked to think of himself as an inventor. His chief hobby was transforming his houses (of which he had several) into medieval castles and fortresses, adding towers, turrets, moats, tunnels, and gateways with slits in them through which you could poke a bow and arrow. He was particularly proud of the steam presses he had invented, which could turn beams of wood into a vaulted roof, like a medieval cathedral. When there was no space left on the roof to build another turret, he would employ engineers to install the latest modern conveniences, such as pipes for running water.

Ada and William were married on 8th July; Ada could not wait to be free of the baleful influence of her mother and the Furies, and become mistress of her own house at Ockham Park. Anyway, soon she would be 21 – which, for her, promised to be a coming of age in more ways than one.

*

On Ada's birthday, Lady Byron asked the newly-weds to visit her at Fordhook – but said nothing of her reasons. Not until they had gathered in the drawing-room to wait for the dinner-bell to be rung by the butler, did she explain why she had invited them.

'Now you are 21,' Lady Byron told Ada, 'it is

my duty to give you the gift that your father left to you before he died. I have never wanted you to see it before as I thought it would remind you of the strange and dreadful history of our marriage, and of your father's disappearance.'

Ada was hardly overwhelmed with surprise at this announcement. Her mother had always promised her that when she was 21 – though not a day before – she would break her silence about her father, Lord Byron. Even so, it was an emotional moment: after saying her piece, Lady Byron was overcome with weeping, and Ada felt distinctly awkward, reminded of the misery her mother had always seemed to suffer from when she had been a little girl.

'I'm sorry,' Lady Byron now burst out. 'Dr King will have to make the presentation,' at which she fled upstairs, clutching her head as if she were in terrible pain.

Dr King walked over to the fireplace

above which hung the picture, veiled by its green-velvet curtain. 'The time has come,' he exclaimed portentously, reaching up to the curtain and swishing it back with a flourish. 'There is your father!'

For the first time, Ada saw a likeness of the man who had been Lord Byron. What did she see? A haughty-looking man wearing a very unEnglish-looking striped turban and an embroidered jacket. He had a small, curling moustache, long, straight nose, shapely lips and burning eyes.

Ada stood in silence for a long time, staring at the portrait as if by looking so intently she could in some way begin to know her father. She realised that she had never imagined what he had looked like – he had been more of a feeling to her. The man in the picture, she decided, didn't look wicked or mad – or especially dangerous. On the contrary, he was smiling. He was, as she had always suspected, devastatingly handsome.

CHAPTER TEN

On 12 May 1836 Ada gave birth to her and William's first child, a son whom they named George after Lord Byron. In the next couple of years she and William had two more children: Annabella and Ralph.

Ada did not much enjoy being a mother. She complained that the constant 'chatter, chatter, chatter' of the children drove her mad. How could she concentrate on her mathematical calculations with all that noise? Sometimes she felt as if her mind was bursting. She thought it must be her mathematical genius trying to get out.

She felt this pressure so intensely that she became ill, unable to eat or sleep. Her doctor, at a loss to find out what was wrong with her, suggested that she should drink a bottle and a half of claret (red wine) every day. At first, Ada did begin to feel better, but not for long. Her hair began to turn grey, even though she was only 25. She complained constantly of having terrible stomach cramps and painful headaches.

William began to think that his wife might be going mad. Despite being worn out with lack of sleep, she persisted in getting up at six every morning so that she could do more work on her calculations before the children woke up. She began to refer to herself as a 'genius'. Then she told him that she wanted to become a poet.

'Poetry, in conjunction with musical composition must be my destiny,' she wrote. 'And, if so, it will be poetry of a unique kind – far more philosophical and higher in its nature than aught the world has perhaps yet seen.'

Maybe, wondered William, Ada was like her father after all – full of sensibility rather than sense, and dangerously passionate. He began to regret that Lady Byron had given them Byron's portrait so that Ada could look at him every day.

He invited Charles Babbage to spend the weekend with them, hoping that the brilliant mathematician would entertain Ada and match her intellectual energy. He was right.

Babbage brought with him a dozen leather cases stuffed to bursting with what he called his 'scribbling books'. He was spilling over with ideas and excitement for his Analytical Engine.

'The Difference Engine can only process numbers in sequences,' Ada explained to William. 'But the Analytical Engine will be able to perform a wide range of complex mathematical tasks that have been set beforehand using punched cards.'

'Punched cards?'

Babbage pulled out from one of his cases a small, framed portrait of an elderly man in breeches and waistcoat sitting in an untidy study, his hand on a large book and a mandolin at his feet. 'A la Mémoire de J.M. Jacquard' was inscribed at the foot of the picture.

'Who is it?' asked Ada.

'This is the man behind my inspiration about punched cards. It's Jacquard, the famous French silk weaver. This picture looks like a pen-and-ink sketch but it was actually created out of silk.'

'But that is impossible – it is so detailed. No weaver could possibly have created such intricate shapes and lines on a single loom.'

'But it is,' insisted Babbage. 'It is made completely of silk, woven by looms that are controlled by punched cards. This one small portrait of Jacquard required 24,000 punched cards all slotting into the loom and each directing it in a different action. I intend to use punched cards in the Analytical Engine to feed in the information that the machine needs to make its calculations.'

'And more than this.' Babbage went on, his eyes burning with enthusiasm, 'I think this machine could actually be operated by steam.'

'But surely an engine that can do all these things would have to be absolutely enormous, far bigger than the Difference Engine?' said Ada.

'I have worked out that when it is completed the Analytical Engine will be about the size of a small locomotive. About 15 foot high, six foot across and 20 foot long. Imagine!' shouted Babbage in his excitement, 'A giant steam-driven calculator!'

Ada could imagine. She felt like her old self again, alive with ideas. She wanted to sort out in her own mind how this could work, how it could be used, how it could change the world.

As Babbage was fond of telling her, 'These machines can show us how miracles happen.'

CHAPTER ELEVEN

Shortly after Babbage's visit, Ada received a letter from him. He had just returned from Turin where he had been explaining the workings of his Analytical Engine to a gathering of Italian philosophers. While there he had met Luigi Menebrea, who had later published a description of the Analytical Engine just as Babbage had described it, and including all of Babbage's calculations. Babbage was delighted with the compliment, but could not read it because it was in Italian. He wanted it translated and published in

English, but with detailed notes, explaining in straightforward language just what an extraordinary invention the Analytical Engine would be.

When Ada received his letter, she felt as though a flame had been lit inside her. She could translate from the Italian – she knew the language well, thanks to her mother's efforts to educate her – but she intended to do more. She wanted to write a commentary as well, explaining *exactly* how the 'Thinking Machine' worked. She wrote a letter to Babbage immediately in which she offered herself for what she was convinced was the most important task of the 19th century.

Babbage's response was to rush down to Ada and William's new house at East Horsley Towers, near Ockham, to deliver Menebrea's book in person. Ada set to work that afternoon.

For the next two years, Ada thought of little else. She worked with a frantic energy, messages and letters flying between her and Babbage;

at times she seemed almost mad in her obsession. She took to calling the Engine her 'child' and was completely convinced that she was a genius, writing to Babbage that 'the more I study, the more insatiable I feel my genius... to be'. On another occasion, she wrote that she was 'thunder-struck' by the brilliance of her translation.

Eventually, in 1843, *Menebrea: Sketch of the Analytical Engine* was published. 'The Analytical Engine weaves algebraic patterns just as the Jacquard loom weaves flowers and leaves,' wrote Ada, as ever making perfect poetic sense out of mathematics. Charles Babbage called her 'the Enchantress of Numbers'.

The book was a sensation and Ada became almost as famous as her father had once been. Imagine how it must have been for the Victorians who first read *Menebrea*. As children, they had lived in a world with no railways, when it took days of being cooped up in a stagecoach to travel from London to Somerset. The electric telegraph, the steam engine, the gas lamps that illuminated the dark were all recent inventions. Now this book, by the daughter of England's greatest poet, explained that it was possible to build a machine that could operate like a human mind.

Some feared that it was an abuse of nature, an outrage against God, to suggest that machines could think. Others regarded it as a magnificent display of man's ingenuity, of the triumph of mathematics. No wonder *Menebrea* made Ada so notorious – especially since women in that era were not supposed to understand science and mathematics, let alone write books about them.

*

Ada revelled in the celebrity that *Menebrea* brought her. For several months, she felt as though the entire world was at her feet. But soon, without the stimulation of spending every waking hour thinking about the Analytical Engine, she began to suffer again from stomach cramps and headaches.

Ada was only 28 years old but she looked much older. Like most Victorian adults, she had lost many of her teeth and she had become painfully thin. Day by day, it seemed, she became weaker and more irritable; unable to ride or even stroll around the garden. But she was still possessed by her passion for numbers. In everything around her, she saw the satisfying patterns of mathematics, and she described the world as a clockwork universe that was wound up by God then left to go through its motions without His intervention.

She believed that her ill-health and her unhappiness must have a scientific solution and she decided that the remedy could well be electricity. In those days, electricity was a recent discovery and people were fascinated by the idea that electricity and magnetism might be used to control the mind and cure madness. Ada feared madness more than anything, believing that this is what had caused her father to be obliterated from her mother's memory.

Among the Lovelaces' neighbours at Ashley Combe in Somerset was an eccentric inventor called Andrew Crosse, who had converted the ballroom of his home, Fyne Court, into a vast laboratory where he worked on experiments with electricity conducted through a huge cable, a third of a mile long, suspended from his apple trees and entering the ballroom through a window. The men who worked for him on his estate called him the 'Thunder and Lightning Man'.

Ada thought Crosse might be just the person to help her investigate the strange workings of the human nervous system – or, more precisely, her own highly sensitive mind. She became fascinated by magnetism, reading copiously and making many trips to Fyne Court to experiment with magnetic charges.

But this new friendship was disastrous. Not surprisingly, the magnetism did little to improve her health; meanwhile, on her frequent visits to Fyne Court, Ada had made fast friends with Crosse's son John, who was also interested in science, but who, for Ada, had another far more insidious attraction: gambling.

The exhilaration of putting money on horse races became yet another new obsession, and before long Ada was heavily in debt, owing hundreds of pounds and borrowing from her mother while pretending that the money was for something else. She was forced to sell all the family jewels to pay her debts, substituting them with fake jewellery that she had specially made so that neither William nor her mother would find out what she had done.

Ada had always loved taking risks and having

adventures, and John Crosse was dangerously exciting to Ada. Before she died, she gave him the only things she possessed that had belonged to her father: Lord Byron's signet ring and his last letter. It was perhaps the most important present she ever gave to anyone.

CHAPTER TWELVE

Ada continued to lose weight and suffer from terrible stomach pain, and by 1850 she was too weak to travel between her homes in London and the country. But there was one journey she knew she still had to make – to see her father's home at Newstead Abbey.

As the twilight gathered on a warm September evening, the Lovelace carriage with its family crest drove up the drive to the house. All that could be seen of the ruined abbey itself was a stone skeleton of ivy-covered arches, with empty frames where there had once been stained-glass windows.

An eerie place, it was surrounded by grassy humps, the site of ancient graves.

Inside the house, (which had been sold to a Colonel Wildman by Lord Byron to pay off his debts), everything had been restored, but Ada could still feel the haunted atmosphere that her tutor William had described to her all those years ago.

She saw the fountain in the cloisters carved with strange and grotesque stone faces, and the griffins and eagles of painted wood in the great hall. In the dining-hall, she recalled that her father had once drunk wine out of a goblet made from the skull of a dead monk – or so it was said.

In the garden, she saw the stone monument that marked the grave of Byron's beloved dog, Boatswain. And she came across a great oak tree where the entwined initials 'A.B.' and 'G.B.' were carved into the trunk – the initials of her father,

George Byron, and his beloved half-sister Augusta.

It was the last trip that Ada was to make. On her return to Great Cumberland Place, near Hyde Park in London, her friend Charles Dickens came and read aloud to her the death scene from his novel *Dombey and Son*. Ada knew that she herself was dying.

William, so sad he could hardly bear to enter her room, left flowers at the end of her bed. At her bedside, bossy as ever, instructing her to write letters, to confess her wrong-doings and to give her mother control over all her papers, was Lady Byron. Ada, rebellious to the last, only gave in when she was too weak to say no.

In her half-waking, half-sleeping state, racked by pain and unable to eat, images from her past raced through her head: a dancer glinting in the candlelight; a portrait covered with green velvet; the dark towers of a ruined abbey; a figure of eight cut into the ice of a frozen lake; a wondrous calculating machine.

On 27 November 1852, Ada died in her sleep, of cancer. She was 36 years old. She was buried next to her father in the Byron family vault at Hucknall Torkard. Her coffin, covered by a violet-coloured velvet cloth, had handles made of solid silver.

Ada's death was mourned by thousands of people – not just because she was the daughter of Lord Byron but also, more importantly, because of her work with Charles Babbage on the Analytical Engine – a machine that we now call

THE COMPUTER

EPILOGUE

In 1980, the first American computer-software language was christened 'Ada' in her memory.

AUTHOR BIOGRAPHY

LUCY LETHBRIDGE IS A FREELANCE JOURNALIST
AND LITERARY EDITOR OF THE TABLET.

WILLIAM SHAKESPEARE
The Mystery of the World's Greatest Playwright
Rupert Christiansen

Everyone has heard of plays like Macbeth and A Midsummer Night's Dream. But why do we know so little about the man who wrote them? Who exactly was William Shakespeare from Stratford-upon-Avon, and why do so many people believe that he was not the person he seemed to be?

This book is an exciting detective story, which goes back over four hundred years to the dramatic events of the reign of Queen Elizabeth I and explores the way that a brilliant and ambitious yound man was caught up in a violent world of murder, revenge and treason.

ISBN: 1-904095-34-8

In case of difficulty in purchasing any Short Books
title through normal channels, please contact
BOOKPOST Tel: 01624 836000
Fax: 01624 837033
email: bookshop@enterprise.net
www.bookpost.co.uk
Please quote ref. 'Short Books'